Marvin Warren

A Solution of Our National Difficulties

Vol. 1

Marvin Warren

A Solution of Our National Difficulties
Vol. 1

ISBN/EAN: 9783337811457

Printed in Europe, USA, Canada, Australia, Japan

Cover: Foto ©Suzi / pixelio.de

More available books at **www.hansebooks.com**

O F

Our National Difficulties,

AND

The Science of Republican Government;

BY A

CITIZEN OF THE UNITED STATES.

———◆———

CINCINNATI:

SOLD BY GEORGE S. BLANCHARD,

No. 39 WEST FOURTH STREET.

OF

Our National Difficulties,

AND

The Science of Republican Government.

BY A

CITIZEN OF THE UNITED STATES.

———— ◆ ————

CINCINNATI:

SOLD BY GEORGE S. BLANCHARD,

No. 39 WEST FOURTH STREET.

TO THE

PEOPLE OF THE UNITED STATES OF AMERICA,

OF ALL PARTIES—LOYALISTS AND INSURGENTS,

NATIVE AND FOREIGN BORN;

WITH AFFECTIONATE REGARD FOR YOU ALL,

TO YOU, AND TO THOSE THAT SHALL COME AFTER YOU,

𝕴 𝕯𝖊𝖉𝖎𝖈𝖆𝖙𝖊 𝖙𝖍𝖎𝖘 𝕷𝖎𝖙𝖙𝖑𝖊 𝖂𝖔𝖗𝖐.

Your most humble servant,

And fellow citizen,

THE AUTHOR.

July 4, 1863.

ADVERTISEMENT.

All profits, both to the Author and Publisher, arising from the sale of this work in the Loyal States, will be expended in giving it free distribution, as far as may be necessary and practical, in the so-called Seceded or Disloyal States. And it is proposed to transfer the exclusive copyright to any person or persons who will give sufficient guaranty that it shall be thoroughly circulated in all accessible parts of the United States, within a reasonable time.

Country Dealers can be supplied by GEO. S. BLANCHARD, Cincinnati, Ohio, and by many other wholesale dealers in cities.

Price, at retail, of this second edition, pamphlet form, 20 cents.

M. WARREN, PUBLISHER.

Bellefontaine, Ohio, Oct. 8, 1863.

ANALYSIS.

CHAPTER I.

PRELIMINARY REMARKS.

CHAPTER II.

PROBLEM I.—WHAT IS THE CAUSE OF OUR PRESENT NATIONAL DIFFICULTIES ?

CHAPTER III.

PROBLEM II.—THE REMEDY FOR OUR NATIONAL DIFFICULTIES.

CHAPTER IV.

CONCLUDING REMARKS.

SOLUTION

OF

OUR NATIONAL DIFFICULTIES.

CHAPTER I.

PRELIMINARY REMARKS.

WHAT IS A SOLUTION?

In the science of Mathematics, or quantities, there are a few plain, self-evident truths called axioms, such as the following: If equal quantities be equally increased, their amounts will be equal; if equal quantities be equally diminished, their remainders will be equal. By the successive application of such plain truths as these, the Mathematician goes forward step by step with absolute certainty, and at length brings out the answer to the most complicated question in the science; and the answer thus obtained, is not correct merely in his opinion, but he absolutely knows it to be so. This is solution.

So in the science of Government, there are a very few plain truths, easily comprehended, and readily assented to by every man, by the proper application of which, the most difficult and complicated questions may be solved with the same absolute certainty as in Mathematics.

What is the cause of our present National difficulties? And what is the remedy to be applied for them? These are the two questions, the solution of which is the object of this little work. It is proposed to solve them by the use of such axioms, or self-evident truths and historic facts as are familiar to all, and often referred to and repeated by the advocates of all parties.

Those who ponder carefully these axioms or truths, and the relation and bearing that each one has upon the subject, will agree that this solution is the only correct one of the two momentous questions before us.

But in this, the utmost care and attention is necessary. There are diamonds in the earth—but they lie not upon the surface to be picked up by the casual observer. Deep excavation must be made—and when the diamond is reached, close scrutiny is required to distinguish it from other earthy substance. So in this solution; the choice truths which pertain to it, lie mingled with a vast amount of other extraneous truths—amongst the whole of which search must be made, and as fast as we discover the objects of our search, one by one, they must be selected and carefully preserved for our use. The difficulty lies not in comprehending the material truths, but in separating them from those that are immaterial, and in rightly applying each one in its proper order and place.

PARTY SPIRIT.

The reason why we arrive at such different and opposite results, in solving our problems in the science of Government, is because we come to the task with minds clogged with party prejudices and passions. The subject is susceptible of the same absolute certainty, as that of Mathematics, and if we would come to its study with minds as free to properly comprehend and apply every principle pertaining to it, as we do in the solution of questions in arithmetic, we would as uniformly agree in our final results and conclusions.

The baneful effects of party spirit cannot be better stated than is done by President Washington in his Farewell Address. Speaking of this spirit of party, he says: "It serves always to "distract the public councils and enfeeble the public administra- "tion. It agitates the community with ill-founded jealousies "and false alarms; kindles the animosity of one part against "another; foments occasionally riot and insurrection. It opens "the door to foreign influence and corruption, which find a "facilitated access to the Government itself through the "channels of party passion."

"There is an opinion that parties, in free countries, are "useful checks upon the administration of the Government, "and serve to keep alive the spirit of liberty. This within "certain limits is probably true; and in Governments of a "monarchial cast, patriotism may look with indulgence, if not "with favor, upon the spirit of party. But in those of the "popular character, in Governments purely elective, it is a "spirit not to be encouraged. From their natural tendency, it "is certain there will always be enough of that spirit for every "salutary purpose; and there being constant danger of "excess, the effort ought to be, by force of public opinion, to "mitigate and assuage it."

The writer of this little work has endeavored to divest himself of all party bias in its preparation; he fully believes he has done so, and asks the reader to come to its perusal with the same spirit of impartiality. There is no good reason why we should hold such opposite views. Surely some, or all of us, are in error, and by reason of this error, our common country has been brought into great peril and disaster. Who will not now make one determined effort to know the whole truth, to reason correctly, and to discover the real evil, though it should be found with his own party, or even with himself?

WHO OF US AT FAULT?

Let no one imagine that in the perusal of this work he will find himself or his party exonerated from fault in the origin of our present National difficulties. On the contrary, although there are great differences in degrees of fault, yet a portion of the fault lies with every party, every section of the country, and almost every citizen.

SLAVERY.

Some there are, who profess to believe that Slavery is a very bad institution; that it is wicked, immoral, impoverishing to the country, and a national dishonor; and that it ought to be done away. Others advocate the opinion that it is ordained of God, founded upon the laws of the Bible; that it is right and honorable, calculated to impart to both races the highest degree of improvement and social happiness, and that it should be extended and perpetuated by the National Government. And still others there are, who think it an evil, but at the same time hold that it should not be done away, for fear of still greater evils that might result.

As these conflicting opinions, with a variety of questions of Constitutional law relating to the same subject, constitute the great theme of distraction amongst us, it may be supposed that this solution will treat largely of these questions; but having gone carefully over the whole solution, the writer is unable to see that the subject of Slavery, in any of these phases, has any place in it. It may be true, as some have declared, that this nation cannot or could not long exist half slave and half free; but whatever truth there may be in this, those who are intrusted with the administration of the general Government have nothing to do with it. The Government should be administered upon the principle of the Constitution, leaving each of the different systems of social and political organization, recognized by the Constitution, to advance in growth, or die out and give place to others, just as their respective merits or demerits may destine them.

EXPLANATION OF TERMS.

Wherever the word *citizen*, or *people*, is used in this solution, let it be understood to mean white citizen or white people. This, however, is not assuming to determine the great question of colored citizenship in this country. But for all the purposes of this solution, it will be sufficient to confine the meaning of the term citizen, or people, to the white race alone.

" THE CONSTITUTION AS IT IS, AND THE UNION AS IT WAS."

The fault lies not in the Constitution. One party of the present day has adopted the correct maxim in this particular. Our fathers have given us a correct chart by which to guide our Ship of State ; and now that we find her ready to founder amidst shoals and quick-sands, it would only increase our danger at this critical moment, to either cast away our chart, or to begin to mark out new courses upon it. There is safety in only one course of action now ; and that is, to turn to our chart, examine it carefully, observe where we have deviated from its course and directions, return to these with the utmost caution, and with the least possible delay, and then for the future adhere to them.

CHAPTER II.

PROBLEM I.—WHAT IS THE CAUSE OF OUR PRESENT NATIONAL DIFFICULTIES?

THERE IS A FUNDAMENTAL WRONG.

It is an axiom in the science of government, that every government must have its foundation. Every government, like every building, is made up of a foundation and superstructure. If any part of the superstructure of a building be removed, the building will be more or less damaged, and rendered less adapted to its use; but if the foundation be taken away, the entire superstructure must fall together in a mass of ruins. And precisely so it is with governments. Whilst it is detrimental to a government to disregard any of its laws, it is even ruinous and fatal to the government itself, to trample upon and violate its fundamental principles, or any of them.

Now we know where the wrong lies from the effect produced. This government of ours has not sustained injury merely in some part or parts of its superstructure. This cannot be. The whole fabric, for years, has been shaken as if by the unseen power of the mighty earthquake, and is even now threatened with overthrow and irreparable ruin. We all know that such results as these can only be produced by some cause at the foundation.

It is plain, then, that in searching for the cause of these difficulties which are upon us, we must direct our attention to the foundation of the Government. First, we must examine carefully, and see what the foundation consists of; and then ascertain how and wherein it has been impaired; or whether, in fact, it was not originally defective and insufficient to answer the purpose. So sure as effect never follows without a cause, so sure shall we find on examination, either that the foundation of this national Government has been in some manner impaired, or else the conclusion is' upon us, irresistible, that it was originally defective and fallacious; or, in other words, either the experiment of our Fathers is about to prove a failure, or else we have ceased to try it.

WHAT CONSTITUTES THE FOUNDATION OF THE GOVERNMENT.

The freedom of speech, the purity of elections, and the sovereignty of the majority, constitute the Foundation of this Government.

By the plan and genius of this Government, the will of the people is the source of all authority in this country. This could be proved by the Constitution, and the teachings of the Fathers, but it is not necessary that it should be proved here in any manner, for no one denies it. It is the first maxim in the political creed, not of any one party, but of all parties, and of the whole country.

This will of the people is absolute in its authority. It rises above presidents, congresses, courts, legislatures, governors, and even above the Constitution itself; for by the terms of that instrument, it is subject to change by authority of the people, and in no other manner. In a word, the people are the final arbiters, by whose authority, either directly or indirectly, every controversy is decided. They constitute the high court of last resort, for the trial of every question of Constitutional law and of public policy, and from their decision there is no appeal.

The people, however, differ amongst themselves upon almost all questions brought before them. Their wills do not generally agree. This makes it indispensably necessary that some rule be established for determining what constitutes the will of the people. For this purpose every citizen is held to be entitled to equal political power with every other, and the will of the greater number, or majority, is taken and held as the will of the people. And this construction establishes the sovereignty of the majority, as a fundamental principle of the Government, for all purposes except for a change of the Constitution, which requires more than a majority, as specified in the Constitution itself.

Although the will of the people is the foundation of all authority, yet this proposition is the mere theory of the subject. Unless there be some laws of action laid down, by which the will of the people can be formed and expressed, the theory amounts to nothing. In order to give effect to the theory, two other things are necessary besides the rule of the sovereignty of the majority : first, the freedom of speech; and second, the purity of elections. Without the freedom of speech, the will of the people cannot be enlightened, or rather no will can be formed; and without the purity of elections, their will cannot be expressed, though ever so well formed and enlightened.

The people of these United States constitute one great legislative body, with the highest powers and responsibilities. What would any legislative body do without the power of free discussion amongst themselves, or the power of voting?

When any subject comes before a legislative body, the first business is the discussion, or consideration amongst themselves; the second is the voting; and third, the declaring of the result, which requires an application of the rule of the sovereignty of the majority. And this is the order in which these three great fundamental laws stand related one to another and to all other laws in this country. True, the people do not vote directly for or against the laws, but they vote for, and elect for themselves representatives, who make and unmake the laws, and this is substantially the same thing.

The voting must have precedence of any application of the rule of the sovereignty of the majority, because without the voting there is nothing upon which the rule can operate. And the discussion must come before the voting, otherwise the people have no will to express by their voting; or, in other words, they come to no understanding amongst themselves upon the subject, and are in the condition of the builders at the Tower of Babel, with a common purpose, but no common counsel.

Here is the foundation of this Government. By the three great fundamental laws, of free discussion, purity of elections, and the sovereignty of the majority, the Fathers designed that every other law should be defined, every difference reconciled, and every right and interest adjusted in a peaceable manner. This was their experiment. Has their experiment failed, or have we ceased to try it? This is the question now to be answered. Have we been maintaining the freedom of speech, the purity of elections, and the sovereignty of the majority, or have we not?

Before we can determine whether we have been maintaining these fundamental principles or not, it becomes necessary to examine carefully and see in what they severally consist. We must, in the first place, see that we understand ourselves, and one another, when we talk about the freedom of speech, the purity of elections, and the sovereignty of the majority. This being done, we shall be prepared to examine into the administration of the Government, past and present, and see whether these principles have been maintained.

FREEDOM OF SPEECH.

Definition of.

The Freedom of Speech consists in the liberty of every citizen, freely to express his opinions, in any manner, on all subjects, and at all times and places, being answerable only for an abuse of the privilege. No one can deny the correctness of this definition, if the whole of it be taken together, including the qualification at the close. The precise extent of meaning, however, that belongs to each of its several parts as they stand thus qualified, is not clear, by any means, without much study and reflection. Let us, therefore, take up the several parts of the definition, one by one, and, by careful analysis, endeavor to ascertain definitely the true meaning of each part, and the whole of the definition.

Who may Exercise the Freedom of Speech.

In the definition already given it is stated that the right of free speech extends to every citizen. The word *citizen*, however, is variously applied. Sometimes it is used to denote any man, woman or child who is a member of the community, and entitled to the protection of the laws. At other times it is used to distinguish such only as are allowed to exercise political powers, and have the privilege of voting. For the purposes of this solution, the meaning of the term may be restricted to this latter class alone; and we need not inquire here, what privileges of speech may or may not be exercised by any except those who are allowed the right to vote.

Amongst those having the right to vote, there can be no distinction or difference in respect to the right of speech. Each citizen voter being entrusted with the same amount of sovereign power as every other, there can be no subordinates, no superiors. It is just as necessary for one to have access to all available means of information as for another; and, in legal contemplation, the opinion or judgment of any one is entitled to as much weight and consideration as that of any other. The right of free speech, then, is, from reason and necessity, inherent in every voter, at least.

Toleration of Opinion.

The word *opinion*, used in our definition of the freedom of speech, must there be taken to mean that which any one claims to be his opinion. We cannot probe the secrets of men's hearts or minds to know whether they really believe that which they affirm.

It makes no difference how false or absurd the opinion may be. The freedom of speech requires that no one shall exercise any prerogative over another in judging between truth and falsehood; and that every one may advocate, not that which *is* true only, but that which he claims to be so. If the doctrines thus advocated by any one are manifestly false and absurd, the advocacy of them will do no harm; and if there be in them any appearance of truth, they should not be suppressed.

The law of free speech is based upon the theory that the people, taken as a whole, are capable of judging between truth and falsehood, when both are fully and freely presented. And this was the principle held by the Fathers, that the advocacy of error could safely be tolerated while the truth is left free to combat it. From this view it is plain that it is incompatible with the law of free speech, to suppress the advocacy of any doctrine or opinion, on the ground that it is false or absurd.

Manner of Exercising the Freedom of Speech.

The freedom of speech includes the Freedom of the Press. Writing and printing are but different modes of speech. Whatever a citizen has a right to declare in person orally, he also has a right to declare by writing, printing and publishing; or by employing others to perform any or all these offices for him. And this implies the right to be secure in the possession of papers, printing presses, types and books, and the inviolability of the right of property in his publications, when being transmitted through the mails or otherwise.

Whatever a man has a right to declare, he has a right to declare by such means and instrumentalities as he himself chooses to adopt. And it is his right to be unmolested in the use of these means, whatever they may be. And let it be understood, that wherever the term *Freedom of Speech*, occurs in this solution, it embraces in its meaning the freedom of the Press, as well as oral discussion.

Subjects of Free Speech.

In this country, by virtue of the present form of our Government, the people are the absolute disposers of every thing. There is no law, no institution, and no interest too high or sacred for them to touch. Restrained they are, it is true, by the constitutions of the several States and of the United States, yet even these, by the terms of those very instruments themselves, are subject to change at the absolute will of the people.

In the Declaration of Independence, our Fathers said, that "Whenever any form of government becomes destructive of these ends," (namely, 'life, liberty, and the pursuit of happiness,') "it is the right of the people to alter, or to abolish it, and to institute a new Government, laying its foundations on such principles, and organizing its powers in such form, as to them shall seem most likely to effect their safety and happiness." According to this theory, the people have at their absolute disposal their highest and most sacred organic laws and institutions. It is true, according to the language of the Declaration, the right of the people to abolish their Government depends upon the contingency that it has become destructive of its ends of securing life, liberty and the pursuit of happiness; but, at the same time, the people are to be the sole, absolute judges of the existence, or non-existence of this contingency, and if they judge wrong, there is no appeal and no help for it.

In recognition of this great cardinal doctrine of the Declaration of Independence, the Constitution of the United States, and those of the several States, have been framed, each with a provision for its change by authority of the people.   It is true, any change in the Constitution of the United States, or of any of the States, in order to be legitimate, must be made in the manner, and by such majorities as are specified and required in those Constitutions respectively.   But when the people proceed in such manner, and by such majorities, as are required by their organic laws, to make changes in the same, they may make any change that they see fit, and their action in so doing is as legitimate and valid as any other that they can do.

If, then, the people have such absolute legitimate power over their primary or organic laws, surely they have no less power over those that are secondary, and created in pursuance of the primary.   And this covers the whole ground.   There are no other laws, known to political organizations, but primary and secondary: and from this it is perfectly plain that the people have absolute legitimate authority over all the laws of the land. They may modify any of them in any manner they see fit, or abolish them altogether and adopt new ones.

And if the people have such unlimited power over their laws, they have no less power over all their institutions.   For every institution is supported by some law or laws; and it would be strange indeed, if the law that supports an institution could be abrogated by the people, and yet the institution itself remain untouched or undisturbed.   Such a thing could not be.

Now the privilege or right of discussion must be co-extensive with the power to make and unmake laws.   This is a self-evident truth.   What is there, then, that the people have not the right to discuss?   That which is constitutional and lawful they must have the right to discuss, because they have power to make it unconstitutional and unlawful; that which is neither constitutional nor lawful they must have the right to discuss, because they have power to make it constitutional and lawful; that which is local they must have the right to discuss, because they have power to make it general; and that which is general they must have the right to discuss, because they have power to make it local; and in every case, whether they will make any of these changes, or suffer all things to remain as they are, must be determined by discussion, and mutual interchange of opinions and views.

The proper subjects of free speech, then, extend to all political institutions, and to all matters and things that are in any manner the subjects of law, or which any one proposes or claims should be made so.   This is carrying the demonstration as far as we have any need of for our present purpose; and it would not pertain to this solution to inquire to what other subjects the law of free speech extends.

When the Freedom of Speech may be Exercised.

The people are called upon frequently, at stated periods, to pass judgment upon both the men and measures by which they are governed. To enable them to do this with justice to themselves and the country, they must have an uninterrupted acquaintance with governmental events as they transpire. True, there are exceptions to this rule; there are plans and doings of the Government connected with its foreign relations and military operations that for the time being are necessary to be kept secret within the immediate counsels of the Government. But there is no necessity at any time, for keeping secret the general purposes of the Government, or the principles upon which it is being administered; but, on the contrary, it is highly necessary that these should not only be plainly declared by the Government itself, at all times, but that the means for an acquaintance with these, be open to every citizen.

There must, therefore, be no interruption in the toleration of the laws of free speech. In peace and in war, the rules of free speech are the same; but the circumstances and facts to which those rules are to be applied, differ very essentially, at different times. It is only necessary, however, that we obtain a clear knowledge of these rules, and we will have no difficulty in making the application under all the varied circumstances that arise from time to time.

Where the Freedom of Speech may be Exercised.

At what places, and to whom, may a citizen declare his opinions? This is an important inquiry. If we consider what the objects and necessities are, for the maintenance of the freedom of speech, it will enable us to understand fully this part of our subject. These objects and necessities are two-fold: first, to insure good laws; and, second, to insure their supremacy. Or, in other words, to insure, first, wise counsels, and second, peace and harmony. How shall these objects be accomplished?

The country is made up of a great variety of interests; and the history of our race shows, that generally, each man is inclined to view every thing in the light of his own interests, with comparatively litte regard for the interests or rights of others. This is accounted for upon principles perfectly consistent with the honesty of all men. It results from the fact that, generally, in this world of labor and anxiety, men find enough to do, to properly care for their own interests and rights, without burdening their minds with those of other people. This is not universally true, but generally it is so. And hence the absolute necessity of continual free intercourse amongst citizens of all the various shades of interests that make up the community of the nation.

Unless this intercourse be kept up, so as to enable each citizen to reason with all his fellow citizens, upon the subjects of his rights, his interests, his motives and his desires, the effect will quickly be seen in mutual bickerings and hatred. This result will follow just as certain, and just as natural, as any other in the moral or material world. And yet it is not because men are disposed to do each other wrong, but simply from mutual misunderstanding.

Where people live together in the same locality or State, this mutual intercourse, and interchange of thoughts and views amongst themselves, is much more likely to be kept up, and more difficult to be prevented, than between citizens living in distant parts of the confederacy ; and hence, so far as the action of the Government is concerned, in the preservation of free speech, much more will be required to be done for its maintenance between the citizens of different parts of the confederacy, than between those of the same parts. Because, looking at the matter in the light of reason, as well as observation, it is plain that a misunderstanding between different sections of the confederacy, is fully as fatal to the peace and harmony of the country, as though it were between the people of the same sections or States.

The freedom of speech, then, does not consist in the privilege of expressing one's views in his own State, nor in his own section of the country, but in all the States, and in all sections and localities of the country, and everywhere, on land and sea, wherever the national flag floats. It does not consist in the privilege of expressing one's views merely to his fellow-citizens of his own State, or his own section of the country, but to all his fellow-citizens of all the States, and of every locality. And the American citizen who has not this privilege, does not enjoy the freedom of speech.

But it will be said that there are some matters of local concern merely, which the people of other sections of the country have no right to discuss in the locality of their existence. There is no greater error than this, and none more fatal. We have already seen, that, by the doctrines of the Declaration of Independence, and the provisions of the Constitution, the people of these United States, as one political association, have power to change even their most sacred organic laws in any manner they see fit. To make that local which is general, and that general which is local; to abolish that which is either general or local, and that which is neither general nor local, to ordain and establish, as either or both, are all acts strictly within the legitimate power of the people of these United States, which they may accomplish by changes in their organic law, if in no other manner. And in all cases, and at all times, the propriety or impropriety, justice or injustice of any and all such changes, is to be determined by mutual counsel and delibration amongst all the people, and not a part.

Moreover, aside from all considerations of organic change, if there be any thing in the laws or institutions of any State, which any citizen of any other State believes to be unconstitutional, or detrimental to his rights or interests, or detrimental to the rights or interests or honor of anybody else, or of the whole country, what is there improper or wrong if such person express his views upon the subject to the people of the State where such laws or institutions exist? Who has authority to say that he shall not do this? The exercise of such a right is neither in conflict with the Constitution of the United States, nor with any State Law or Constitution that is itself Constitutional. And the more such free expression is exercised and encouraged between the several parts of the country, the more permanent will be our peace and prosperity.

The freedom of speech is no local right, nor can it be, consistent with the peace and safety of the country or government. Where there is no freedom of speech, the people become ignorant of their own interests. All their earnings and resources are at the disposal of a few, and this creates a monopoly for corrupting the entire nation and government. Being shut out from the rest of the world, and no ray of light permitted to come to them, unless tinged by the coloring of their politicians, the people form false ideas of the doings and motives of their fellow countrymen in other parts, and of the Government under which they live, and it becomes perfectly easy to incite their passions of hatred, revenge, insubordination and rebellion.

Let the freedom of speech be destroyed in a single State of this Union, and we will have a power, the natural antagonist of Republican Government, the baneful influence of which will be felt, to some extent, throughout all the others. Let the same be done in a number of them, constituting even any considerable minority of the whole, and we will have a combination of corrupt influences, against which, the friends of free government, may hope in vain, to contend successfully for many years.

Then let it not be said that it is no concern of the people of one State whether the freedom of speech be preserved in the other States or not. To destroy the freedom of speech in any State, or in any locality, is an injury to the people, not of that State or locality merely, but of the whole country. It is the right of every citizen, not only to have the means of information himself, but to demand that every other citizen, in all other States, as well as his own, shall enjoy the same privilege; for the safety of his Government, and the safety of every interest and right that he holds dear, depends upon it.

Abuse of the Privilege of Free Speech.

All that we have said upon the subject of free speech, must be taken with this qualification, that there should be no abuse of the privilege. The abuses into which we are liable to fall, consist in the uttering of scandal, or matter treasonable, or inciting to the commission of crime, or the violation of law.

The law of scandal, so far as it relates to individual detraction, being generally quite well understood and settled in this country, and not having any immediate bearing upon the subject of this solution, need not be discussed here at all, further than to observe, that no one has any right so to exercise the liberty of speech, as to commit unnecessary or malicious detraction against the character of another, anywhere, at any time, or under any circumstances whatsoever. And this rule holds good in respect to candidates for office, and those in office, as well as other persons.

Treason against the United States, is defined by the Constitution, as consisting "only in levying war against them, or in adhering to their enemies, giving them aid and comfort." If then the country be in a state of war, there are many ways in which a citizen may be guilty of treason merely in the use of speech, either by speaking, writing, printing or publishing. Every word that conveys valuable information to the enemy in respect to the position, strength or supply of armies; or in respect to the plans of the military authorities of our Government; or any word that would deceive or mislead our own authorities in respect to the position, strength or plans of the enemy; or any use of speech that hinders our Government in the raising of armies or supplies, or aids the enemy in doing the same, is giving aid and comfort to the enemy, is treasonable, and constitutes an abuse of the freedom of speech.

Of course it makes no difference whether the war is a foreign or domestic one; only in this, that if it be a domestic one, the opportunities for doing these things, to the advantage of the enemy, and to the injury of our own Government, are much greater than in case of a foreign war. Nor does it make any difference whether our Government, or the enemy, is justified in the cause of the war, or in its beginning or purposes.

The act of "levying war" against the United States is treason. To levy war is to make war, or begin it, and this may be done by grand forcible resistance to the acts of the Government in the performance of its functions, as well as by onward aggressive attack. And if war be actually levied by either mode against the Government, every citizen by whose counsel or advice the same has been done, is guilty of abetting treason, in the abuse of free speech.

To counsel, advise or encourage the violation of any law, is also an abuse of the freedom of speech. And it matters not whether the law be of a civil or criminal character, or whether designed for public or private protection. Nor does it make any difference whether the law be established by legislative, executive or judicial authority, provided the authority be that of the United States, or of any State acting as a member of the confederacy of the United States. Every decision of a Court of Justice, and every rule, regulation or proclamation of the Chief Executive of the United States, or of any State, or of any Executive Officer, acting under the authority of either of these, in the performance of his duties, is a law, the violation of which no man has any right to instigate or advise, any more than those that emanate from the legislative branch of the Government, and are found upon the Statute Books of the country.

Nor does it make any difference whether the law be good or bad, constitutional or unconstitutional. For after all, these characteristics are but matters of opinion, and if each man is to be governed by his own opinion in these things, then no law will have any force. If any law is, in our opinion, unconstitutional, or in any thing unjust or unwise, this is a sufficient reason for us to seek, in the lawful and constitutional way, to have it repealed or abrogated, but is no justification for its violation, or for counseling the same. To discuss the laws is one thing, to "Spit upon, despise, and trample" upon them, is quite another.

It must also be observed, that a person may abuse the freedom of speech by instigating resistance to authorities or the violation of law, without directly counseling the same to be done ; and this may be either from his very manner and in the use of such language as fires the passions of men ; or it may result more from the circumstances of the excited state of the public mind, combined with his criminal neglect to season his speech with suitable precautionary advice.

The Freedom of Speech has long since been Destroyed.

Having now examined into the law of free speech, so far, at least, as it relates to political discussion, and having seen in what the law consists, we are now prepared to examine into the past and present condition and usages of the country, and see whether this law is and has been maintained amongst us or not. If every citizen is permitted freely to express all his opinions upon all the laws and institutions of the country, and upon all political subjects, at all times, in all places, and in any manner that he sees fit, subject only to answer for any abuse of the privilege, then we have political freedom of speech, but otherwise not.

Now, how is this, and how has it been heretofore? Has every citizen of each and every State been permitted to mingle freely and safely in the society of every other State and everywhere, and to all his fellow-citizens of those States, to express all his opinions upon all the laws and institutions of the country, and upon all political topics? Every one knows that it has been far otherwise. For forty years the subject of Slavery has been one of the leading subjects of political interest, and intimately connected with almost all other subjects of national politics. During all this period, the interest upon this subject between the Northern and Southern sections of the country has become more and more intensified, and from 1850 to 1860, it was in fact the all-absorbing question, that swallowed up every other in our National politics. And yet, strange to say, in proportion as the subject became great in interest and importance, the freedom of speech was curtailed between the North and the South upon it, until finally, for some years previous to the breaking out of the present rebellion, only one side of the question could be advocated at all, by anybody, to any available extent, in the fifteen slave States of the Union.

For all practical purposes, in arraying one section of the country in deadly hostility against the other, the destruction of free speech was complete. It is true, the people of the North were permitted to declare their own sentiments in their own section of the country, but, as we have already seen, this does not constitute the freedom of speech. No citizen of the United States enjoys the freedom of speech, unless he has this privilege, not only in his own section of the country, but in all other sections. Nothing short of this privilege, enjoyed by all the citizens of the United States, constitutes a national free speech; and nothing short of this, will answer any purpose of saving the country from anarchy, or the Government from overthrow.

The truth, then, is simply this, that so far as relates to the freedom of speech, the first one of the three great fundamental principles of the Government as laid down by the Fathers, we have discarded their foundation, and have been trying to build upon something else, or upon nothing. And hence we have accounted, at least in part, for the calamities which are upon us.

It matters not now, by whose fault it was that the freedom of speech was destroyed amongst us; it is sufficient to know, for our present purpose, that it was destroyed.

THE PURITY OF ELECTIONS.

Definition Of.

We come now to consider the second great fundamental law of our Government, the Purity of Elections. This consists in the *free exercise, by every citizen voter, of the right to vote strictly according to his own judgment, without restraint from violence, and without influence from fear or favor.* Of course the freedom of speech, however well maintained, will avail nothing without the purity of elections.

Restraint by Violence.

To exercise any restraint by violence, over a voter, in respect to the casting of his vote, is such a palpable violation of the principles of Republican government as to need no process of reasoning to show the true character and criminality of such an act. This right of freedom on the part of the voter, implies also every right that is incident and necessary to it. The right of personal safety and liberty in going to the polls; and the right to confer with his fellow-citizens for the purpose of putting candidates in nomination, and the preparation of ballots, are all rights just as necessary to be exercised by him, as the right of choice amongst candidates, when at the polls.

Have these rights been maintained in our country, or have they not? Occasionally we have had riots here and there, by which ballot boxes have been destroyed or taken possession of, and by armed or violent intervention, citizens have been prevented from voting according to their choice. Most of these occurrences have taken place in some of the large cities. But far the most extensive riots that have ever occurred of this kind in the country, took place at the election in the Territory of Kansas, on the thirtieth of March, 1855, by which, there is no room for doubt, that in many places acts of the most shameful violence were committed, and, probably, the grand result was effected thereby. All these cases of riots at elections, however, are but individual instances, and have not been so wide spread and general as to affect seriously the stability of our institutions.

There is one species of restraint, however, by acts of violence over the elective franchise, that became general throughout most of the Slave States for several years previous to the breaking out of the Rebellion, and was of such character and extent, as necessarily to impede the operations of our Republican principles, and affect materially the stability of the Government. This was the custom of preventing Abolitionists from making nominations and from voting for the candidates of their own choice in the Slave States. Without assuming to decide any thing either in favor of or against the principles of these Abolitionists or Republicans, (by whatever name they may be called,) one thing is certain, and that is, whether their principles were right or wrong, they had the same right to sustain them at the ballot box, as any other citizens had to sustain theirs.

Corrupting by fear of Insurrection.

According to the first principles in the science of government, there must, in all governments, be a sovereign power. This sovereign power is lodged in different places, according to the form of government. Sometimes it is placed in the hands of one class, and sometimes in the hands of another; sometimes it is lodged with one man, at others with many; sometimes its locality is determined by hereditary succession, at others by election; and sometimes it is in part elective and in part hereditary. But under all these forms, and every other, the sovereign power must be the controlling power, otherwise it is not sovereign, and is not the government.

It is perfectly consistent with the character of the sovereignty of the country to allow itself to be petitioned and remonstrated or reasoned with, but when it comes to matters of force, it must prove itself the strong prevailing power. And if it yields in the least to intimidation or threat, this is precisely the same thing in effect, as though it were already subjugated; and in fact this is subjugation. By its yielding, it acknowledges its own imbecility, and the superiority of some other power within its own jurisdiction. One yielding is an invitation to another threat, until threats very soon become the order of the day; they multiply on every hand; the language of rebellion becomes as common as any other; and whatever the government attempts to do, it is insultingly, and continually cautioned of the precariousness of its own existence and power.

This same principle runs through all government. In school or college government, it is the same. No common school teacher can suffer himself to be intimidated into a departure from his own rules and regulations in a single instance, without losing the control of his school. The teacher may be mild in his government, listen to the wants and wishes of his pupils, and even sport with them, all perfectly consistent with his dignity and authority. But in any issue of power or authority, that any of them may make, or threaten to make with him, in the regulations of his school, he must prevail, or his authority and usefulness in that school are at an end; and it matters not whether he, or they, are right in the particular thing concerning which the issue is made. If any of us should go into a school, and hear the teacher threatened on every hand with resistance, in case he should attempt this, that, or the other, we would say at once, he is no governor there, and is powerless to fulfill the objects of his employment. Precisely so, it is, with all government, including State and National. In every case the government must be the strong controling power, sustaining itself far above all contempts or menaces arising within its jurisdiction.

The sovereign power of a country has no right to yield to its motives of fear from menaces of domestic resistance; and if it does so, it acts unworthy of its high trust. Such yielding is but the prelude to anarchy and public danger, and the government that does it, commits a great wrong upon the country of its jurisdiction, and upon each of its citizens. Every citizen has a claim upon the clear judgment of the sovereignty, unbiased by motives of fear or favor, upon the pure questions of justice, of sound policy and of constitutional law. No government has any right to be moved by any other considerations than these, and it is highly criminal, on the part of any citizen, to attempt to influence it by any other motives. No other influences or motives can be justified by any circumstances of real danger from domestic violence, for if there be danger of this kind, it will not be diminished by any manifestation of fear on the part of the government, but quite the contrary.

Now, in this country, if indeed we have any sovereign power at all, it is with the people. Every voter bears in his own person a share of the sovereignty, and the mode of exercising his sovereign power is by his vote. To intimidate a voter, then, is to intimidate, in some measure, the sovereign power of the country. To say to a voter, that in case this or that be done in political or govermental affairs there will be insurrection, rebellion or disunion, and to say this with a view to influence a voter in the casting of his vote, is the very worst mode of corrupting elections. And if the voter yield to this influence, he acts upon principles as base as the corrupter himself.

What shall we say then of the man who stands up before an assembly of the sovereign people and tells them that he is a Democrat or Republican in principle, believes in the right and practicability of government based upon the will of the major-

ity, and then, in the same address, tells them that if the majority determine thus or so, their authority will be put at defiance
and overthrown? Are not his doctrines and teachings in plain
conflict with themselves? How much of consistency can be
accredited to the man who tells the assembled masses of the
people that he has great confidence in their intelligence and
integrity, and then, at the same time, tells them that these
endowments of theirs are to be held subordinate to that base,
cowardly fear, that is to be inspired by those who dare to talk
flippantly about resistance, secession, disunion, or separation of
the East from the West, and the North from the South. What
is such a man but a wholesale corrupter of elections? And
yet, strange to say, a very large share of the electioneering
capital of the entire nation, for the last forty years, has consisted
of this very stuff; and stranger still, hundreds of thousands of
us have been influenced by it in our votes.

No wonder the sovereignty of this country has become con-
temptible and weak in the estimation of its enemies, when its
friends thus acknowledge its imbecility. The people of this
country owe nothing to the men who meditate rebellion. They
owe everything to their own united and determined action in
support of their own Government and laws; and this united
action, while it continues, is fully sufficient to carry them tri-
umphantly through every contest of domestic violence.

What is right? What is wrong? What is constitutional?
What is unconstitutional? These are the only questions with
which the voter has to do in the determination of his vote.
With these soundings of alarm of danger to the Union, he has
nothing to do, further than to inquire from whence their origin,
and who it is that dares to meditate resistance to that mighty
sovereign power, a portion of which he bears in his own person.

One thing we should not fail to observe in reference to these
alarmists about disunion. They seldom acknowledge any design on the part of themselves to engage in rebellion; not
they, but it is somebody else; and this somebody else is alluded
to in terms so indefinite as to leave it altogether uncertain who
is meant. Now if there is any danger to the Union, then somebody meditates rebellion; and whenever this alarm is sounded,
we should lose no time in demanding of the alarmist what his
authority is for giving it, and who the evil designer is; and if
he fails to give satisfactory answer to these inquiries, we should
hold him as the culprit, or one of the culprits, in whose heart
dwells the foul, sacrilegious purpose of raising violent hands
against the sovereignty of this free Government.

We have now seen that in two ways the purity of elections
has been to a great extent taken away in this country: first by

denying to the people of anti-slavery sentiment the privilege of the free elective franchise in the Slave States, and second, by the influence of fear upon the citizens, everywhere, for the safety of the Union and Government. Whilst these are the only means by which the purity of elections has heretofore been so far destroyed as to effect materially the stability of the Government, we should do great injustice to the subject if we should leave the impression that they are the only means by which the same can be done. No doubt new modes will be resorted to, from time to time, for accomplishing the same end, conforming ever to the points where the people are least watchful of danger, thus impressing our minds, ever afresh, with the truthfulness of the adage, that "eternal vigilance is the price of liberty."

Having now seen that the foundation of the Government has long since been removed, so far as it was constituted of the first and second great fundamental laws, to wit, the freedom of speech and the purity of elections, we now pass to an examination of the third and last one of those laws, namely, the sovereignty of the majority.

SOVEREIGNTY OF THE MAJORITY.

What it Is.

Sovereignty means supreme power, majority means more than half; literally, then, the Sovereignty of the Majority means the supreme power of that part of the citizens, constituting more than half of their whole number. Now it is seldom that more than half of the voters of the United States, or of any State, can agree fully in regard to any thing, and this gives rise to the necessity of taking the word majority in this connection in a qualified sense; and under some circumstances the will of a less number than the absolute majority is taken as the will of the majority. This is what is properly called the constitutional majority, and arises from unavoidable necessity in the application of the principles of republican government in practice.

In the election of officers it is rare that the first choice of the majority of voters rests upon any one man. Hence, usually, the candidate having the highest number of votes is deemed to be elected, whether his number of votes be a majority of all or less.

Where there are a large number of candidates, it is plain, that in this manner, one might possibly be elected by a small vote, who would be quite unfit for the trust. For this reason the Constitution requires that in the election of the officer of the highest importance, (the President), a different and more precautionary method be followed. This officer is chosen by electors, who are themselves elected by the people; and a majority of all these electors is required to make the choice. And if no candidate receives the vote of such majority, then the House of Representatives, the members of which are elected by the people, are to choose the President from the three candidates having the highest number of electoral votes, the representation of each State being entitled to one vote only, and the votes of a majority of all the States being necessary to a choice. And in choosing the Vice President, who is the President's alternate, a similar precautionary method is adopted.

Now it is very clear that whatever expedients are resorted to in the election of any officer, there is absolutely no will of the majority generally in the matter; for it seldom happens that the will of the majority accords in favor of any one candidate. Even in those cases where a majority of the votes are cast for some one candidate, there is usually no such accordance; but the vote is cast by virtue of the party nomination.

And again, if we had no laws except those that are accorded to us by the absolute will of the majority, we should have but few laws; for it is seldom that any law is passed, that is precisely in accordance with the will of a majority of all the people, or even of the legislative body that passes it. In the first place, the will of the people cannot be taken directly in the passage of laws, but it must be done through the medium of those elected by them, which is an imperfect mode of representation, though the very best that can be adopted.

Every act of Congress, every proclamation of the President, every order given, or regulation prescribed by him, or by any one of his ten thousand subordinates, every decision of the Supreme Court of the United States, is a law; and by the theory of our Government, each and every one of these laws is founded upon the will of the people; and yet not one-tenth of the questions involved in the expediency of these laws are ever presented to the minds of the people at all, prior to the election of the officials by whom the same are adopted. New and unlooked for exigencies, questions and subjects of momentous consequence, often arise during a term of office, upon which the official must act, without the means of consulting the judgment of a majority of his constituents, and, in some cases, with but little time to consult his own.

The Judges of the Supreme Court of the United States, are not elected by the people, but are nominated by the President, and confirmed by the United States Senate. And when so chosen, they hold their offices for life. Thus the laws given by the Supreme Court, are often founded on the will of the majority of a former generation, if indeed they may be said to be founded upon the will of a majority at all. We see, then, how imperfect our representative system is, throughout, in expressing the will of the majority.

But even if the representative system were perfect, and each and every official were a perfect exponent of the sentiments of the majority of his constituents, yet in matters of legislation, it is impossible to make the absolute will of the majority any guide at all, for the reason that it often happens, and probably oftener than otherwise, that the majority of the legislative body does not accord or agree in respect to the laws that are passed by it. It not unfrequently happens, that a law is passed by a legislative body, that is so far from being approved by a majority of its members in every one of its provisions, that it has not such approval of a single member. Every one takes some exception to it, but the exception taken by one is not the exception taken by another, and a majority do not concur in the taking of any one exception, and hence each and every member, of that majority by whom it is passed, vote for it, not because it meets his approval altogether, but simply because he deems it better than to pass the subject over without action.

We see, then, that imperfection characterizes this our system of representation and majorities, in all its parts. But it cannot be otherwise. The absolute will of the majority, as a rule of action, in the selection of officers, and in the making and unmaking of laws, is a thing utterly unattainable. Hence by the Constitutions of the United States and the several States, or most of them, a system is adopted that probably approximates as near to perfection as is practicable, and by which is adopted what may be called the constitutional majority. This system may not be as perfect as it might be. But surely, to say the least of it, it approximates so near to the greatest attainable degree of perfection, that any failure or difficulties in the success of our institutions, cannot be attributed to this imperfection, and hence no occasion arises here, for any objection to the doctrine of "the Constitution as it is, and the Union as it was."

Sanctity of all Laws.

Notwithstanding some of our laws are approved by the absolute majority of the people, and some by the constitutional majority only, there can be no distinction between laws, in respect to authority, sanctity, or inviolability. The whole system of laws is bound together in such manner that all must stand or fall together. It is utterly impossible to administer those that are approved by the absolute majority of the people, without also administering those that are approved by the constitutional majority only. To neglect one of these, is to neglect the other, and to oppose one, is to oppose the other. If it be anti-republican to oppose the one, it is equally anti-republican to oppose the other.

And so in respect to the relative authority of the laws emanating from the different branches of the Government. It will not do to say that a decision of the Supreme Court of the United States, or an order or proclamation of the President, is of less authority than an act of Congress. The executive, legislative, and judicial branches of the Government are all dependent upon each other; and to trample upon the authority of one of these, is to trample upon the authority of the whole. To weaken one, is to weaken the whole. Much has been said in this country of the danger of encroachment of one branch of the Government upon another. But in a country like ours, where all three branches of the Government are under the control of one sovereign power of the people, this is the least of all our dangers, if indeed it may be said to be any danger at all. The great danger with us, is, that we do not yield sufficient obedience and support to any branch of the Government.

The truth is, we have never sufficiently learned the importance of adhering to the inviolability of our own laws. We ought to understand that to trample upon any law, however unimportant in itself, that has been adopted under the authority of the Constitution, is to trample upon the Constitution itself. The laws are dependent upon the Constitution, and the Constitution upon the enforcement of the laws. All our laws, good and bad, great and small, State and national, primary and secondary, executive, legislative and judicial, are bound together by one grand chain of dependence; and it is impossible that one jot or tittle in any wise fail, without affecting the whole.

Our laws not only have a mutual dependence, *per se*, amongst themselves, but they all emanate from one great authority, namely the people, and to call in question the authority of one, is to call in question the authority of the whole. No good man can say of a bad law, that it is bad, and therefore I will not regard it, nor of any unconstitutional law, that it is unconstitutional, and therefore I will not regard it, nor of a needless law, that it is needless, and therefore I will not regard it, without setting an example before bad men, to do and say precisely the same things in respect to those laws that are good, constitutional and needful. Every truly loyal and good man, will yield ready and cheerful obedience to all laws. If any of them are bad, unnecessary or unconstitutional, in his judgment, he will seek by the constitutional and lawful mode to have them abrogated; but he will set up no independent judiciary of his own, to determine them unconstitutional, nor countenance any disobedience or resistance on the part of others.

How different from this are everywhere our customs and practices. It is true in many instances we manifest great zeal in support of the laws; but this is often more from the force of our own inclination in the particular instance, than from any reverence for the laws.

To illustrate our meaning, let us take a single instance. Suppose we go into the State of Ohio, the society of good order and republican principles. We find here written upon the statute book of the State, "that it shall be unlawful for any person or persons, by agent or otherwise, to sell, in any quantity, intoxicating liquors to be drank in, upon, or about the building or premises where sold," and that if any person shall offend against the provisions of this law, such person shall be punished by certain fine and imprisonment. For nine years this law has stood upon the statute book of that State, plainly written, and well known to every person in it, as the clear, settled will of the majority; yet, if we go into almost any village in the State, we can easily find one or more places where this law is violated a hundred times a day, and that, too, by the countenance and assistance of a hundred different men in buying, for the purpose for which the law forbids any sale to be made. Now, although it is true, no one but the seller incurs the penalty of the law, yet every one who buys under such circumstances, countenances and aids in the violation, and manifests the same disregard for the sanctity of the law as the seller himself. And this is a common practice throughout nearly all parts of the State; the persistent determination to violate the law being so general and so great as to baffle all efforts of the friends of the law for its enforcement.

Now the men who manifest such contempt for the law, call themselves Republicans and Democrats. But are they so? What is a Republican but one who believes in the right and authority of the majority to prescribe laws for the government of the whole, and maintains this principle by his influence and example? And what else than this is a Democrat? If we would maintain a Republican or Democratic Government here, we must maintain the sovereignty of the majority: or, in other words, we must maintain our own laws, and in this, make no compromises with our own individual or collective inclinations or tastes.

There are in almost every State, sundry laws, like this Ohio liquor law, lying almost a dead letter upon the statute book, although plainly the expressed and settled will of the majority.

The spirit that actuates those men who persistently violate them, is the spirit of lawlessness, constituting the germ of insurrection, rebellion and anarchy. And this spirit is not confined to the dominions of Slavery; it is everywhere, East and West, and North and South; it is in our midst, and in our very hearts. Everywhere, and in everything, it intrudes itself, and strives for the mastery. It is the spirit of anti-republicanism, against which we must wage a perpetual warfare. offensive and defensive. And the strong weapons of our warfare are not so much the organization of parties, with hallowed names, and the promulgation of rigmarole platforms and resolutions, as in clearly understanding a few plain elementary principles, and applying these in everything we say and do.

Compromises.

Anarchy and despotism are two opposite extremes, equally to be avoided and guarded against. In all republics there is a time for the people to direct the Government, and a time for the Government to direct the people. The people's time is at the election, that of the Government afterward. Between elections the people should carefully study, and freely discuss, the acts of their Government and its officers; but at the same time they should attempt no direction or control. The reason of this is, because at the election is the only time when the voice of the sovereign majority can be distinguished from that of the minority.

Now we must advert again to the elementary principle in the science of government, that in every government, no difference what its form or kind, there must be a controlling power. What has already been said upon this cardinal subject, on pages 24 and 25 of this solution, applies here in full force, and it would be well for the reader to turn back, before proceeding any further in the perusal of this work, and refresh his mind once more with a clear view of the nature and necessity of this great principle as there set forth.

Where there is no controlling power, there is no Government; and where there is a controlling power, that power constitutes the Government. There is no exception to this principle. Go where we will, into any association or organization of mankind, or, if you please, into the regions of the damned, or into the society of just men made perfect, and everywhere we shall find that the principle holds true. There never was an exception to it, and never can be. Republics form no exception to it; but on the contrary, the principle holds as true in regard to these, as in regard to governments of any other form. Republics differ from other governments, not in the essential principle of sovereign power, but in the locality or lodgement of the power.

There can be, in the very nature of things, but one controlling power at the same time over the same jurisdiction, and in respect to the same subjects of government. There may be two powers existing at the same time, each assenting to what is done by the other; or if differing in anything, yet not essentially so, and thus for years, harmony and prosperity be preserved under the reign of the two. But when circumstances arise bringing these powers into collision, when the test comes, which surely will come sooner or later, that is to determine whether of the two is to abandon the great essential principles constituting the basis of its existence and authority, then will be seen which of these powers really constitutes the goverment; which of them is really sovereign, and which subordinate; which of them it is that really exists by virtue of its own powers of self-preservation, and which exists by the sufferance of the other.

In the United States, we flatter ourselves that we have a Republican Government. If this really be so, then the will of the constitutional majority is sovereign amongst us, in all matters of national concern. And if the will of the constitutional majority be sovereign, then the will of no constitutional minority is or can be sovereign; but in any and every issue or conflict, between the constitutional majority and the constitutional minority, the former will and must prevail. This is the very test of republican institutions.

Now suppose a national election has taken place, and a Congress assembles, representing the will of the constitutional majority, in favor of the adoption of a certain measure. The measure is brought before Congress in the form of a bill; and it is ascertained, and becomes notorious everywhere, that there is a clear majority of each House in its favor, and that the President is ready to approve it. But during its pendency the minority bring forward and propose some modification. The measure and its modification are both discussed long and thoroughly. The majority are inflexible in their judgment, and are still bent upon the passage of their measure. But, as a last resort, the minority say, if their modificaton is not accepted, it will result in the dissolution of the Union; and by this means a sufficient number of those favorable to the original measure, are influenced to vote for the modification, to secure its passage into a law, and defeat the original bill. Now where is the sovereignty of our majority? It is no more. It is gone; subdued; subjugated. The will of the majority is no longer sovereign, but subordinate. Once it has been menaced into obedience to the will of the minority; and what has been done once, can be done again, and again, and as often as the minority see fit to present the same alternative. Where now is our republic? Its great essential principle is taken away. And yet this is compromise. Precisely the kind of compromise that was introduced into the legislation of the country a little more than forty years ago, upon the plea of saving the Union. Never was there a greater error, or one followed by cosequences more deplorable.

There have been three compromises in our country, each of which was effected in the manner above stated. And although the historian may not have stated in this same light the origin of the acts of Congress constituting these several compromises, yet they were all originated substantially upon the principle above stated; that is, for the purpose of saving the Government and Union by concilliating those who had become disaffected. It is by no means every compromise that has any thing dangerous or objectional about it. Compromises of some kinds are very common and necessary in the business of legislation. It is only against those that are entered into for the purpose of saving the Government or Union by concilliation that we here raise any objection.

In 1820 there was a majority in Congress, who, according to their own judgment, were favorable to admitting the State of Missouri into the Union in no manner except as a free State. But for the purpose of saving the Union and preserving the peace, is was agreed that it might be admitted as a slave State, with the condition annexed that all other territory belonging to the Louisiana province, and north of the parallel of 36 degrees and 30 minutes, should be forever free. This was the first time in the history of the country that the majority made humble obeisance to the minority; the influence of which obeisance upon the morals of the whole nation has been plainly felt from that time to the present.

Hence it is that we hear so much cautioning about the safety of the Union, which means precisely this: that the majority must be exceedingly cautious what they do, otherwise the minority will resist and overthrow their authority. And this same humble respect for the wishes of the minority, we are told, must be our leading motive, tempering our action in every thing we say and do. Our own opinions of right and of wrong, of constitutional law and of sound policy, are of some little importance, it is admitted, in determining our action; but when the Union is in danger, that is, when the minority threaten it, then it is said we must throw aside our own opinions, and conform to their every demand in order to save it. This kind of teaching is directly antagonistic to republican or democratic principle.

Again in 1833 the second compromise to save the Union took place. The tariff upon some articles of importation, as established by the majority, was too high to suit the best interests and wishes of the minority, and a portion of this minority, the people of South Carolina, placed themselves in an attitude of resistance, and declared themselves absolved from further association in the Union, in case any effort should be made to enforce the tariff, laws as then existing, amongst them ; and many others, also, in other States, deeply sympathized with them, and stood ready to aid the insurgents so soon as the issue should be brought to the test of military force. There were two plans proposed, for meeting this extraordinary exigency, by the Government. The first was from Andrew Jackson, then President of the United States ; which was, to enforce the laws at every hazard and cost. The second was from Henry Clay, then a member of the United States Senate ; which was, to concilliate the disaffection by a gradual reduction of the tariff.

Unless the writer of this solution has reasoned wholly in vain, the plan proposed by President Jackson was right, and that of Senator Clay, radically wrong. The first was founded upon republican principles, was calculated to promote public confidence, public security, public morals, and the stability of our noble Government. The second was anti-republican, and naturally tending to demoralization, to anarchy, insecurity, and the instability not only of the Government, but of every interest, public and private.

We do not pretend to say whether the tariff itself was right or wrong, nor does it matter a whit, when the great essential principle of the sovereignty of the majority was put in jeopardy. And it is a most singular fact, worthy of note, and very instructive with all, that the great leader in this doctrine of enforcement was the chief representative of the free trade policy ; whilst the author of the compromise reduction, was none other than the champion of high protective tariff.

In 1850 there was a third compromise. The Territory of California applied to be admitted as a free State into the Union ; there was a majority of each House in Congress favorable, upon principle, to her admission in this manner ; but it must not be done without a compromise, otherwise the Union was again to be destroyed. And a compromise ensued. California was admitted as a free State, but as a consideration for this the Northern people accepted the present fugitive slave law, and the abandonment of their part of the benefit under the Missouri compromise ; or at least such, was the construction afterward given to this last compromise, as to result in such abandonment. And now for the third time, as was supposed, all vexed, dangerous questions being fully and finally settled, the Union was forever established, upon the unchangeable principles of concilliation and friendship, beyond the power of any disturbing element again to bring it into peril.

But alas! Only ten years more transpire, and the dangers appear as great as ever, and greater. In the election of Mr. Buchanan, the Northern Democracy now feel that they have been betrayed; and there are some matters of principle connected with the government of the Territories upon which they desire to have a better understanding with their Southern brethren, and without which understanding, they feel that there is no chance of success of the great National Democratic Party in the presidential contest into which the country is about to enter. These things are stated by Northern Democrats in their national convention at Charleston; but it is all in vain. Forty years before, the Southern Statesman had assumed that the union of these States was a thing in their hands, to be disposed of at pleasure; and this assumption had been recognized and conceded in three several acts of Congress. And now how could they themselves doubt the fact.

Never before in the history of the country had circumstances been so favorable for successfully testing the reality of the thing which had been so long only assumed and recognized in both the Government and politics of the country. Never before had these southern politicians their iron heel so completely upon the neck of free speech, and of course never before did they hold such complete sway over the blind passions of their own masses, to arouse them at pleasure, beyond the power of Government, or the Northern people to interfere. The administration of Mr. Buchanan, without his design it may be, had been an instrument in their hands for shaping events to suit their purpose of disunion. Should an administration now intervene, not ruled by their counsels, whether Democratic or otherwise, the favored moment would be lost.

Southern politicians could no longer rule the country by deception. As a last resort, therefore, they said plainly to their northern brethren in convention, give us slavery protection in all the territories, beyond interference by territorial or other authority, and we will then be content, but not otherwise. The reply was, we cannot thus eat our own words at the north, and our people will not sustain us if we do; and the result will be a grand defeat of the National Democratic party. It was then and there that the great National Democratic party, and the great nation itself, ceased alike to answer any purpose for southern politicians, and they determined on destroying both. Those of them having the authority to speak, so declared, in the private councils of the convention.

Nothing was being lost, however, in the way of preparation, whilst Mr. Buchanan was President, especially so long as these southern men could deceive that functionary, in reference to their real purposes, and the mutual friendly relation that had long existed between him and them enabled them easily to do this. They could have no objection, therefore, for the time being, to put on the semblance of loyalty, go through the forms of another presidential election, and perchance throw the election into the House of Representatives, and there, by some bargain, secure the candidate of their own choice. But even in this event, there was no intention on their part of remaining in the Union, but on the contrary, the only object they had in securing a president, was to enable them the more easily to get out of it; for they could no longer hope to control the legislative branch of the Government, and their power within the Union, to rule the Government upon their own principles, was essentially broken.

Countrymen: these compromises to save the Union, are a terrible delusion. The present awful sufferings and slaughter, and bereavement, are the fruits, in part, of those same compromises. The Constitution establishes one great compromise to which alone we can adhere with safety. This compromise is a very simple one, easy to be understood, and above every other, it is pre-eminently just and right. It is simply this: *the will of the majority is the law.* Every other compromise that can possibly be suggested comes in direct conflict with this, and tends to the destruction of both the Constitution and the Union. The man who is not satisfied to abide by this compromise under all circumstances, and in its application to every thing, but seeks to set it aside or evade it, in its application to some things, is an enemy alike to the Constitution and the Union, and should not be entrusted with any political power, not even the right to vote. Such a man may deceive himself, and perhaps honestly think that he is a friend to the Union; but his acts will tend to evil none the less for all that.

WE HAVE ABANDONED THE EXPERIMENT OF OUR FATHERS.

At the beginning of this chapter, its purpose was stated to be, the finding out of the cause of our present national difficulties. And the result of our investigation is simply this, we find we have departed from all the first principles of the government as instituted by the Fathers. Our national free speech, the purity of our national elections, and the sovereignty of our national major ty, have all been abandoned long since.

A huge wall of separation has been raised for more than fifteen years between the northern and southern sections of the country, prohibiting free discussion entirely. In one-half of the Confederacy, people holding the sentiments of the majority of those in the other half, are not permitted to vote at all according to the dictates of their own judgments, and have not been for the last fifteen years at least. At every returning election, the sovereign people are every where and constantly told that they must not decide thus and so by their votes, or the Union will be destroyed. And when the election is over, and the people's representatives assemble in Congress to legislate for the country, these also are constantly told that they must not legislate thus and so, or the Union will be destroyed. And the President also, who is one of the chief representatives of the people, is constantly threatened with resistance if he attempts to do this, or that, or the other. These threats of resistance, and dissolution, constitute the basis of every compromise, and for a long time have been the chief arguments, if arguments they may be called, by which the destinies of the country have been controlled.

Now these things all show nothing else than a state of utter political demoralization, totally destructive of the first principles of the Government, and if it be not anarchy itself, it is the sure prelude to it. No wonder that we are involved in difficulties. These calamities that are now upon us are no evidences against the experiment of the Fathers, for we have not been trying their experiment for many years. We have no evidence as yet that the foundation of the Government, as laid by the Fathers, is bad, or unworthy of our full confidence, for we have not been building upon that foundation, but upon something else, or, perhaps more properly speaking, upon nothing at all. True we have all the time had the semblance of republican government. We have had the form, and a mixture of the principles. But this will not do. If we would give fair trial to the practicability of republican government, we must build wholly upon republican principles, and discard everything else. We all know how vain a thing it is to erect a building, one-half upon the rock, and the other half upon the sand. Far better to place it wholly upon the sand, and far better still, to place it wholly upon the rock.

It is not slavery that has brought upon us these difficulties; nor is it the tariff; or any question growing out of either of these, or any other difficult question whatever. In the absence of the issues heretofore presented, others would have arisen equally difficult and distracting in their nature. It is for the want of free speech, purity of elections, and the sovereignty of the majority, that we are visited by these calamities. Without these fundamental principles, as a basis of operations in a republic, the plainest questions become difficult; and those whose interests are one, are made to hate each other with deadly hate; and, with a will, to pour out each other's blood like water, without the slightest cause. But let these fundamental principles be restored, then, although we shall have seasons of political excitement, yet there will be no blood shed; although we shall have difficult and distracting questions to dispose of, yet the intelligence and patriotism of the people will be fully sufficient for the task, of doing this, and doing it too, upon the principles of substantial justice and sound policy. And those who do not believe this, do not believe in the practicability of republican government.

CHAPTER III.

THE REMEDY FOR OUR NATIONAL DIFFICULTIES.

THE FOUNDATION OF THE GOVERNMENT MUST BE RESTORED.

The cause of our National difficulties is the removal of the foundation of the Government; and the only remedy is to restore that foundation. Something more than eighteen hundred years ago, one spake as never man spoke, and said, that a certain "wise man built his house upon a rock; and the rain descended, and the floods came, and the winds blew and beat upon that house, and it fell not, for it was founded upon a rock." And there was "a foolish man which built his house upon the sand; and the rain descended, and the floods came, and the winds blew and beat upon that house, and it fell—and great was the fall of it."

Now, the political and social elements, like the material, must have their conflicts. There must ever be storms of political excitement, from time to time, and there is no help for it. In fact, these are indispensably necessary for the purification of our political atmosphere; and to attempt to prevent them is worse than idle. But one thing we can do. We can adopt the course of the wise man in the parable, and secure well the foundation of our building; and then let the storms come—they will do us no harm. Let us have uninterrupted freedom of speech, purity of elections, and the sovereignty of the majority, and then, whatever may betide us, all will be well.

Before the foundation of the Government can be fully and permanently restored, there are a few things that the people must do, and a few others that the Government must do. And these duties, respectively incumbent upon the people and the government, we will now consider separately.

WHAT THE PEOPLE SHOULD DO.

Before we can have our republic reinstated upon its pure principles, we, the people, must cease to deprecate the agitation of political questions. We must no longer talk about the evils of agitating the slavery question, or of any other question. We must rather encourage and foster the universal agitation of all questions in which the people have any interest. We must exactly reverse our maxims in this respect. And so far from looking upon the agitation of any question as dangerous to our institutions, we must understand that the very first thing necessary and indispensable to the preservation of our liberties and our free government, is the unrestrained liberty of free discussion of all questions, at all times and places, and by all our citizens.

The very fact that a question is exciting in its nature, shows that the people regard it as one of interest to them ; and the greater the interest, the more exciting it will be, and all the more necessary that the people debate it well, and come to a correct knowledge and a mutual understanding amongst themselves upon the subject. And it is necessary that the discussion should be permitted to conform itself to the nature of the interest. If it be a question of interest between the North and the South, then this very fact makes it peculiarly necessary that between these two sections of the country its discussion be unrestricted.

It is true, one may so discuss any question as to perpetrate an abuse of free speech, and produce a result tending to dangerous consequences. But the laws of free speech, and the rules concerning abuses of the same, are alike applicable to the discussion of all questions ; and it is worse than idle gibberish to talk about the dangerous character of certain questions.

And, again, we must cease to disparage our own sovereignty, by acting as the trumpeters of those who are incessantly sounding alarms of danger to the Union, and crying out for compromise. We must, many of us, reverse our maxims upon this subject also ; and instead of talking so much about saving the Union by compromise, we must say, *the will of the majority, it shall be enforced.* We must cease, also, to aid in or countenance those disgraceful acts of violence in the Slave States, whereby the purity of elections has been destroyed ; and we must permit each of our fellow citizens to enjoy the same right of voting according to the dictates of his own will and judgment, as we claim for ourselves.

In a word, we must, with united voice and influence, discountenance every act, every practice and doctrine that even tends to the destruction of free speech, purity of elections, or the sovereignty of the majority. We may differ about slavery, about tariffs, about banks, about internal improvement, and about every thing else, but about free speech, purity of elections and the sovereignty of the majority, there must be no difference amongst us, and there can be no difference amongst those who are truly democratic or republican in principle.

WHAT THE GOVERNMENT SHOULD DO.

Surely, we ought not to multiply our laws ; already we have too many and those too long and prolix. We stand in great need, however, of three very simple laws, all of which could very properly be incorporated in one short act of Congress, and be entitled, *An Act to preserve the Constitution and Union of the States.*

The first of these laws should define the freedom of speech—as already done in this solution—and then provide for punishment, by imprisonment in the penitentiary, of any person who shall hereafter do any act with intent to hinder another in the exercise of such freedom, or consequent upon the exercise of such freedom.

The second of these laws should provide a similar punishment for any person who shall do any act of fraud or violence, with intent to prevent any lawful voter from voting according to his own choice, or consequent upon so voting, or to influence such person in the matter of his vote, especially in the election of all United States officers.

And the third of these laws should provide, that any person shall be punished in the same manner, (by imprisonment in the penitentiary,) who shall hereafter threaten, in any manner, either directly or indirectly, to make insurrection against the laws or authorities of the United States, under any circumstances or in any contingency whatever; or shall intimate or declare that such insurrection is likely to be made by any other person or persons, without at the same time stating reasonable facts upon which to base his opinion, and implicating, as far as he is able, those who meditate the insurrection.

If this National Government would give to these three laws a national sanction, a national adjudication, and a national enforcement, it would effectually guard the freedom of speech, the purity of elections and the sovereignty of the majority, from those encroachments which have been practiced heretofore, and be a complete remedy for all our present National difficulties; and had these measures been adopted ten years ago, they would have saved us from the dire calamities which are now upon us.

CONSTITUTIONALITY OF THESE PROPOSED LAWS.

This Government cannot be maintained without the establishment and preservation of the freedom of speech, purity of elections and the sovereignty of the national majority. And none of these fundamental principles of the national government can be preserved unless by the exercise of the powers of the national government for that purpose.

Principles that lie at the foundation of the government, and upon which the government is dependent for its very existence, cannot be left at the mercy of local influences and casualities with any safety. And if the government of the United States

has not itself the power to guard and maintain these fundamental principles, then it has not the power of self-preservation or self-defense. And if it has not the right of self-defense,
to maintain its own existence against every power and influence
tending to destroy it, (except the authority of the people acting
in the manner prescribed by the Constitution for organic
changes,) then it has no right to exist, and is no legitimate
government. The very fact, then, that the government of the
United States is a legitimate government, (which no one denies,)
clothes it with the powers of self-defense and self-preservation;
and without any express provision of the Constitution it would
have full power to maintain the fundamental principles of its
existence.

But the framers of the Constitution have not left this power
to rest solely upon the natural, inherent right of self-preservation; but by express terms the power is given in the Constitution of the United States, as we shall discover by examination
of that instrument.

Before proceeding to study this Constitution, however, with
reference to any question of power or meaning, it is necessary
to consider one peculiar characteristic that distinguishes that
instrument from all other Constitutional or Statutory law.
This characteristic is its exceeding brevity. It is wonderful
and instructive to take in hand this Constitution of the United
States, and reflect how vast and innumerable are the rights and
interests regulated and preserved, or intended so to be, by a
law of so few words. In every thing we do our action is
restrained by it; and wherever we are, at home or abroad, on
land or on sea, amongst our own citizens or foreigners, we are
under its protecting ægis.

And these rights and interests thus protected, are not those
of individuals only, but of communities, of States and Territories. Nor are they confined to a few persons, but extend to
all persons that dwell in this vast empire of freedom, compris-
ing a large share of the finest portion of the earth, and
absolutely unlimited in its resources. And yet this mighty
machinery of rights and interests is regulated by a law, that,
for extent of words, may well be compared to a child's primer.

This brevity of the supreme primary law, renders it easier
to be understood by persons of ordinary education and reading,
and its preservation is an object of great importance. Such a
Constitution, framed by a convention of modern law makers,
would probably contain five or ten times as many words; and
this constitutes one objection to the convening of any convention
for its revision, lest, by so doing, this brevity might be to some
extent, if not wholly, destroyed.

Now, in studying this instrument, we must not expect to find the respective rights and duties of the government and people pointed out in each one of the ten thousand specific relations and circumstances in which they arise, but we must take the general terms as we find them, and by our own reflection, make the application ourselves.

The preamble to the Constitution declares the objects of making the same in the following language: "We, the people of the United States, in order to form a more perfect union, establish justice, insure domestic tranquility, provide for the common defense, promote the general welfare, and secure the blessings of liberty to ourselves and our posterity, do ordain and establish this CONSTITUTION for the United States of America." Most signally have the framers of the Constitution failed of all their objects, unless they have given to the National Government the power to guard the freedom of speech, purity of elections, and its own sovereignty, or in other words, the sovereignty of the majority.

But they have not failed in this. The Constitution provides that "Congress shall have power to provide for the common defense and general welfare of the United States."[1] This provision confers all necessary power upon the legislative branch of the Government, for the purpose above mentioned. Nothing is plainer, than that under a republican government, there can be no permanent general welfare without a national free speech, purity of the national elections and the sovereignty of the national majority. Reason, as well as experience and observation, teach this. If the national government has not the power to preserve these things, then it has no power to provide against mutual misunderstanding, jealousies, hatred, revenge and civil war. And, moreover, any government, whether republican or otherwise, that has not the power to guard its own sovereignty against contempt, will not long have power to do any thing.

Now if Congress has power to pass laws for the preservation of free speech, purity of elections, and the sovereignty of the majority, then the other two branches of the Government have the power, and are charged with the duty of performing their respective parts for their adjudication and enforcement. For the Constitution further provides, in regard to the duties of the President, that "he shall take care that the laws be faithfully executed."[2] And in defining the powers of the judicial branch of the Government, it is provided, that, "The judicial power

---

1 Constitution, Article I. Section 8.—First Clause.
2 Constitution, Article II, Section 3.

shall extend to all cases in law and equity arising under this Constitution, the laws of the United," &c.[1]

There is still another ground of constitutionality for a national law, providing for the maintainance of free speech and for defending the purity of elections against violent restraint or interferance. This is the incidental power and duty that arises in guarding the sacred rights of personal security and of private property, with which the general Government is charged, and than which, no more responsible trust is committed to its hands.

It is provided in the Constitution, that "The right of the people to be secure in their persons, houses, papers, and effects, against unreasonable searches and seizures, shall not be violated;"[2] and that "No person shall be held for a capital or otherwise infamous crime, unless on a presentment or indictment of a grand jury, * * * nor shall be compelled in any criminal case to be a witness against himself, nor be deprived of life, liberty or property, without due process of law."[3]

And further, "In all criminal prosecutions, the accused shall enjoy the right of a speedy and public trial, by an impartial jury, of the State and district wherein the crime shall have been committed, which district shall have been previously ascertained by law, and to be informed of the nature and cause of the accusation; to be confronted with witnesses against him; to have compulsory process for obtaining witnesses in his favor, and to have the assistance of counsel for his defense."[4]

Upon careful consideration and reflection, it will be seen that these several provisions of the national Constitution guard three points of danger to the citizen. First, that his person and property shall not be interfered with by mobs, nor in any manner without lawful authority; second, that his person and property shall not be interfered with, under the forms or pretense of lawful authority, but without fair legal procedure; and, third, that his person and property shall not be interfered with, in any manner, however lawful and fair in the form of procedure, for frivalous, unjust and untenable causes. Altogether, these provisions go to the full extent of securing each individual in the enjoyment of his great natural rights—"personal security," "personal liberty," and "private property"—pointed out by Sir William Blackstone, the illustrious commentator upon the laws of England;[5] and referred to also in the Declaration of Independence, as the right to "life, liberty and the pursuit of happiness.

1 Constitution, Article III, Section 2.
2 Amendments, Article IV.
3 Amendments, Article V.
4 Amendments, Article VI.
5 Blackstone's Commentaries, Book I; 129.

Now every violation of the right of free speech involves also a violation of one or more of these natural, constitutional rights of personal security, personal liberty and private property. It cannot be otherwise. If a citizen be at any time or place prevented or hindered from the proper exercise of the freedom of speech, either in speaking, writing, printing or publishing his opinions, it must be done by a violation of the right of personal security, personal liberty or private property. Without this there never was, and never can be, a violation of the right of free speech. It follows then of course, that if these sacred guarantees of personal security, personal liberty and private property, contained in the national Constitution, were carried out and enforced, the right of free speech would be carried out and enforced also.

And this is also substantially true in reference to the purity of elections, so far as these are liable to infringement from violent and unlawful means; that is, so far as they have been effected by mob violence, without any color of legal authority; and these have constituted one of the leading instrumentalities by which the purity of elections have been destroyed, especially in the Southern or cotton growing States. If, then, the guarantees of the Constitution were enforced, not only would the law of free speech be fully sustained, but the purity of elections would, to a very great extent, be restored and maintained; and these two results would follow as a necessary and unavoidable consequence.

Now the question arises, upon whom does it devolve to carry out, and enforce, these guarantees of personal security, personal liberty and private property, found in the national Constitution? Most certainly, and clearly, upon the national Government, and upon no one else. The Constitution confers no powers upon any other Government, body politic, or corporate, or upon any individual or other authority except the general Government, to do any thing whatever. The compact of the Constitution was not in the least a dispensing of powers to States, Territories, or other local organizations, nor yet to individuals; but, on the contrary, it was a surrender by these of certain powers to one general government, for the accomplishment of certain objects specified in the preamble. In what plainness and simplicity do we see this set forth, by glancing for a moment at the beginning of each of the three articles of the Constitution, establishing respectively, the legislative, executive and judicial branches of the Government. These are as follows:

"ARTICLE I. SECTION I. All legislative powers herein granted, shall be vested in a Congress of the United States, which shall consist of a Senate and House of Representatives."

"ARTICLE II. SECTION I. The executive power shall be vested in a President of the United States of America."

"ARTICLE III. SECTION I. The judical power of the United States shall be vested in one Supreme Court, and in such inferior Courts as the Congress may from time to time establish."

It is as plain, then, as the English language can make it, that all legislative authority created by the Constitution is vested in Congress; all executive power is in the President, and all judicial, is in the Supreme Court of the United States and such inferior Courts as Congress may establish.

Now every power of Government is either legislative, executive or judicial; these constitute the summary of all Governmental authority. And when these are all given out, as is here done, then there remains no more power to be conferred anywhere. The Congress, the President, the Supreme Court, and such inferior Courts as Congress may establish, constitute the Government of the United States; and not a single act, great or small, is authorized by the Constitution to be done by any official, employe or other person, unless by authority of one or more of these three heads of Departments of the National Government.

Nor is it necessary that any powers should be conferred any where else; for upon these three branches of the General Government, is conferred full power to enforce every guaranty of personal right, and every other provision contained in the Constitution. By the Constitution it is provided that "The Congress shall have power to make all laws which shall be necessary and proper for carrying into execution * * * all powers vested by this Constitution in the Government of the United States, or in any department or officer thereof;"[1] also, "To provide for calling forth the militia to execute the laws of the Union."[2] It is made the duty of the President to "preserve, protect and defend the Constitution of the United States;"[3] and, "to take care that the laws be faithfully executed."[4] and to enable him to do this, he is made "Commander-in-Chief of the army and navy of the United States, and of the militia of the several States when called into the actual service of the United States."[5] And further, it is provided, that, "the judicial power shall extend to all cases in law and equity arising under this Constitution," and "the laws of the United States."

1 Constitution, Article I, Section 8.
2 Ib.
3 Article II, Section 1.
4 Article II, Section 3.
5 Article II, Section 2.

The powers, then, of the National Government for enforcing every provision and guarantee of the National Constitution are complete and ample. The Fathers are not chargeable with inserting in this instrument guarantees of safety and protection to the citizen, without providing any power for their enforcement, merely to deceive him, and betray him into snares fatal to his liberty and safety.

How is it, then, while the National Constitution provides that "the right of the people to be secure in their persons, houses, papers and effects, against unreasonable searches and seizures, shall not be violated, and while the national government is so plainly clothed with the authority and charged with the duty of enforcing this guarantee, that thousands of persons, houses, papers and effects have been searched and seized, for no other reason than because the persons so searched or seized, or whose property was so searched or seized, had expressed opinions adverse to a certain institution of the country and the laws that support it, and yet no act of the general government put forth for redress? Have we not already seen, in the early part of this solution, that the right of free expression of opinion upon all the laws and institutions of the country, at all times, in all places and in any manner, is a right not only inherent in every citizen of a Republican government, but that this same right is the very first principle and chief corner stone of such government? And can any thing then be more "unreasonable" than to search or seize a citizen, or his property, because he exercises this sacred right? While the national Constitution provides that "no person shall be held to answer for a capital or otherwise infamous crime, unless on a presentment or indictment of a grand jury," nor "be compelled in any criminal case to be a witness against himself;" nor be "deprived of life, liberty or property without due process of law;" and that " in all criminal prosecutions the accused shall enjoy the right to a speedy and public trial by an impartial jury, * * * to be confronted with witnesses against him, to have compulsory process for obtaining witnesses in his favor, and to have the assistance of counsel for his defense;" and whilst this same Constitution makes it the duty of the National Government to enforce one and all these guarantees to the protection of every American citizen, it is remarkable, indeed, that this same government should have stood by unmoved, as though it were a disinterested party, with full knowledge of the fact that for a long series of years each of these guarantees were being habitually violated in thousands of instances throughout one-half of the confederacy. But we all understand why these things were done, and why they were suffered to be done. It was in order that the freedom of speech and the purity of elections, in every thing touching the institution of Slavery in the Slave States, should be destroyed; an object that could not possibly be accomplished while these guarantees were being maintained. But by their destruction the object has been attained most completely; and our present difficulties and sufferings are but the natural fruits of this departure from the plain letter and spirit of the Constitution.

By virtue of the powers surrendered by the several States, and by the whole people, in the formation of the national Constitution, it is provided that "this Constitution, and the laws of the United States which shall be made in pursuance thereof, * * * shall be the supreme law of the land, and the judges in every State shall be bound thereby, any thing in the Constitution or Laws of any State to the contrary notwithstanding."[1]   All that is needed, then, to put a stop to these flagrant violations of the National Constitution, is for Congress to enact adequate penal laws, against them, and then, when acts are committed in violation of these penal laws, the offenders could be prosecuted therefor in the United States Courts.   And should any State pass laws infringing in any manner the guarantees of the National Constitution, every case arising in the State Courts for the enforcement of such laws could, if necessary, be reviewed in the United States Courts, and such judgment pronounced as to give effect to the Constitution of the United States and the laws enacted under it.

There is an impression upon the minds of many, that it is the legitimate business of the general government to attend only to those things which pertain to the general interests of the whole country, and that it does not behoove the National Government to stoop to look after the rights of individuals. This is a great error.   It is one of the objects of the National Government, as stated in the preamble of the Constitution, to " establish justice;" and it is in pursuance of this object that the guarantees of personal rights are incorporated in the Constitution, and these guarantees are for the protection of all the people, and of each man, woman and child, constituting the people.

It is the duty of the National Government to protect the rights of its citizens against violation by foreign powers, and, if need be, to engage in war for the protection of a single citizen.   And it is under precisely the same obligation to protect its citizens or subjects against domestic violation, as against foreign.   The guarantees of the Constitution are absolute, and provide for the protection of each and all the

---

1 Constitution—Article VI.

people, at all times, in all places and against every violation, from whatever source, or under whatever pretext it may come. At home and abroad, on land and on sea, each and every one is to be secure—secure against foreign or domestic interference; against violations at the hands of one or many, against State or United States authority; against violations under the forms of law, or by infuriated mobs. To be secure, absolutely, in person and property, in their individual and collective capacity, is the right of each and all the people; and it is the duty of the National Government to see that this right is everywhere, at all times, and at every cost and hazard, rigidly maintained.

We do not pretend that the National Government should interfere for the redress of every violation of the rights of person or property between citizens—by no means should this be done. The State Governments have, or should have, full power to do this by virtue of their own constitutions, and it is much more convenient and appropriate that it should be done by them. But in those cases where the State Governments are either unwilling or unable to protect the rights of their own citizens, or the rights of other persons coming within their jurisdictions, the National Government should interpose its authority for this purpose, even although it should be necessary to do it in opposition to the power of the State Government.

For individual protection within the States, the National Government should only exercise its powers in those cases where the State Governments fail to do so. Now, aside from the incidents of war, the State Governments generally have enforced the rights of personal security, personal liberty and private property, except in those things wherein it has been necessary to disregard them for the purpose of destroying the freedom of speech and the purity of elections, and hence it is proper that for the present the action of the civil authorities of the National Government should only be so far exercised, for the further protection of individual rights, as is necessary to reinstate these two fundamental principles of the Government.

But, it will be inquired, is it the duty of the National Government to stand between the authorities of a State and one or more of its citizens? Most assuredly it is, whenever the constitutional rights of either of these parties is violated by the other, and that other party is without any other redress. Each citizen owes to his State Government his allegiance and support, and his State Government owes to him the observance and protection of all his personal rights. But when either of these parties, disregarding the obligations due to the other, with strong hand invades the rights of that other, then it is for the

National Government to interpose its power for the protection of the weaker party. Hence these guarantees of individual rights in the National Constitution, one of the leading objects of which, was, to protect the citizen against the encroachments of his State Government. And hence, also, the counter provision, in the same instrument, that "The United States shall guarantee to each State a republican form of Government, and shall protect each of them against invasion, and on application of the legislature, or of the executive (when the legislature cannot be convened), against domestic violence."[1]

There are certain constitutional rights and obligations existing between each State and its citizens, between the citizens of each State, between the several States, between each State and the citizens of every other State, and between the citizens of different States; and high over all these, the National Government is established, a great supervisory power, whose duty it is to take cognizance of all that is done between these parties, to protect the weak against the strong, and to redress every violation of constitutional right, where redress is not otherwise attainable.

NO OTHER REMEDY, THAN TO RESTORE THE FOUNDATION OF THE GOVERNMENT.

There are many who think that Slavery is the great disturbing element of the country, and that if we could by any means get rid of this institution, nothing would any longer remain to endanger the Government. These persons are greatly in error. There is no such institution as this in Mexico; and yet the existence of that Republic has ever been extremely precarious, from domestic causes—much more so than our own. Others there are who think that if Slavery could be nationalized, and admitted without restraint or prejudice throughout all the States and Territories, wherever slaveholders should find it profitable or convenient to settle or go in transit, that the great cause of disaffection would be taken away, and that nothing would any longer mar the unity of the people, or disturb their Government. These persons, also, are in great error. If they will look candidly, into the society of the Slave States, they will discover there elements of discord and of disintegration that will surely work dismemberment amongst themselves just as certain as they ever become an independent people, at peace with the rest of the world.

Some there are who have full faith in the virtues of some party to save the country, and believe that if the people would only give control of affairs to such party, at every succeeding

---

1 Constitution, Article IV, Section 4.

election for all time to come, that this would secure the perpetuity of our republic and institutions. These persons are greatly at variance amongst themselves, in reference to which party it is that possesses this peculiar virtue; but in one respect they are all alike, being, every one of them, in great error. Every political party that ever did exist, has been made up of two elements—patriotism and demagogueism. And it is no difficult thing to see how one of these elements may preponderate to-day, and to-morrow the other, in any party; and nothing tends more to the preponderance of the latter named element than to keep the party continuously in power.

Some there are whose whole attention is fastened upon some party, which they think is the great source of all mischief and danger, and believe that the perpetuity of the Government depends wholly upon the destruction of such party. These, also, are at variance amongst themselves in respect to which party it is that should be destroyed; but are all, equally in error, in reference to the consequences that would follow upon the destruction of either. Others there are who think that if the present rebellion can be effectually subdued, and the leaders made to pay the penalty of their lives, that this will be such a vindication of the power and practicability of our republican Government, as that no further dangerous attempts will be made against it. Of all errors that prevail, none are greater than this.

The three simple remedies, already proposed, freedom of speech, purity of elections, and sovereignty of the majority, will, if adopted, save this Government and country, and impart prosperity to both, just as long as we continue their application, though it be a thousand years, or ten thousand, should the present order of nature continue so long. These three things are the instrumentalities by which the Fathers designed every evil should be remedied, every error corrected, and every difference reconciled, and they are fully adequate to these purposes.

But without these remedies, it matters but little what may be done, there will be no more permanent peace and prosperity for us. We may abolish Slavery, or nationalize and perpetuate it; call into power whatever party we may, or abolish all parties; give the helm of State into the hands of wise men, or fools; good men, or bad; hold our country as one, or divide it in twain, or twenty; theorize and devise as we may upon the policies of peace or war; raise mighty armies and navies; fortify on land and on sea; tax ourselves to the exhausting of all our substance; and sacrifice ourselves by hundreds of thousands upon fields of crimson gore—yet all will be in vain. The prosperity, power and glory of the great American Republic has already departed beyond retrieving, unless we return to first principles, to the "Constitution as it is, and the Union as it was;" or in other words, to the freedom of speech, purity of elections, and sovereignty of the constitutional majority.

The men of this generation may live to see this rebellion and war cease; the Slavery question settled; the abolitionists of the North and the slaveholders of the South united together in the greatest harmony and friendship—we have already seen stranger things than these—but neither we, nor our children, will see permanent peace and prosperity here, unless it be established upon the basis of these first principles of the Constitution. Peace we may have, but so soon as the country recovers from its exhaustion, war will again be renewed. The Slavery question may be settled, but a hundred others there are, any one of which may spring up in a day, and become just as difficult. The South may be united to the North in the strongest feelings of nationality; yet the West may separate from the East—a separation that geographically would be much more natural, easier to consummate, and more difficult to prevent—and then divisions, and subdivisions, and reunitings will succeed each other without end.

Without a return to first principles of the Government, it is impossible to tell precisely what is in the future for us; but it is quite safe to predict that insecurity, instability, weakness and disgrace will characterize our course. It is not likely that we shall be either united or separated; we shall have neither Monarchy, Aristocracy or Republic, but a continual strife between the principles of all these, with ever varied and uncertain result. On the contrary, however, if we now unite as one man, in returning to the pure principles of republicanism, the freedom of speech, purity of elections, and the sovereignty of the majority, as instituted and practiced by the Fathers, and these faithfully adhere to and apply, in the settlement of all our difficulties, and in the adjustment of all our rights and interests, then, bright and glorious beyond description, will be the future of this great country.

CHAPTER IV.

CONCLUDING REMARKS.

THE PRESENT CIVIL WAR.

ALL must agree, that upon the whole, the present war is one of neither profit nor honor to the country, or to the institutions of our Fathers. Every person who is truly a friend to these free institutions bequeathed to us, must be anxious for the termination of this bloody strife, as early as possible. The question is, how shall it be made to cease ?

The principles already established, by the reasoning of this solution, furnish a ready answer for this question. The sovereignty of the constitutional majority, is the principle upon which peace must come to us, if it ever comes at all. A peace not having this principle for its basis, would be no peace. The constitutional majority is our sovereign. This sovereign authority speaks to us through the Government at Washington City. Let us all obey. If we do this, those of us in arms against the Government, will lay them down, and the war will cease at once ; or for want of this action on their part, then those of us who are loyal will unite all our efforts under the direction of the Government, to compel them to do so until the object is accomplished, and then the war will cease. The process is simple indeed, and he that runs may read and know his duty in the crisis. It is all a delusion, or something worse, for any man to pretend to be a friend to peace, unless he is in pursuit of it upon the plan marked out by the Government. That plan may not be the best, but at the very worst, it is surely better than any number of conflicting ones.

EMANCIPATION AS A WAR MEASURE.

To discuss the subject of emancipation, in any of its forms, would be a departure from the objects of this work. It is proper to observe, however, that it is the duty of the Government to put down this rebellion at any and every cost of life and property that may be necessary. Though it should be admitted that slaves are property, yet surely they are no more sacred than other property.

Circumstances may justify the burning of a whole city, where half the people are loyal. And circumstances may justify the destruction of the institution of Slavery in a part or a whole of the Slave States, though half of the slaveholders deprived of their slaves should be loyal. Now, it is not likely that one slaveholder in ten, in the districts affected by the President's proclamation, is loyal. But, after all, whether the circumstances of justification exist, for the emancipation measure, is, like every other act of the Government, a fair subject for discussion amongst all the people, guarding, however, against any abuse in the instigation of resistance.

MILITARY ARRESTS.

"The Constitution as it is," requires the President to "take care that the laws be faithfully executed." This provision is unqualified in its terms. There is no limit of time, or place, or manner. Of course, in seasons of great rebellion, like the present, he cannot do it to perfection, but at all times and places he is to accomplish it as near to perfection as he is able. In peace and in war, in loyal and disloyal districts, this is to be his care.

Now, suppose it to be a time of peace, but the President has reliable information that certain persons, in some section of the country, are laboring successfully to set on foot a gigantic rebellion, with a view to set at defiance and overthrow the laws. Or suppose a rebellion actually exists in one section of the country, and he has information that in the loyal part of the country there are persons who are aiding or abetting it. What is the duty of the President under such circumstances? If either or both of the other branches of the Government, the Courts or the Congress, should interpose their authority, and stop these men in their work of treason, then, of course, the President would have nothing to do in the premises. And, in fact, if the other branches of the Government always could and would take care to see that the laws are faithfully executed, then there would be no necessity for this provision of the Constitution, requiring the President to do it. But in cases like the above, where for any cause whatever, the other branches of the Government fail to do this work, then surely the President has it to do; otherwise the words of the Constitution have no meaning.

But the question arises, how and by what instrumentalities is he to do the work of executing the laws? The Courts may be open for the transaction of business, but they are no instruments in his hands for any purpose. They are not subject to his command. They constitute one separate branch of the Government and he another. The Courts are efficient in their own way and time in taking care for the faithful execution of the laws, but what they do, is done independent of the President's authority, and without his command or instigation. When it comes the President's time, then, to act for this purpose, what are the instrumentalities with which he is to work? Plainly he must use the instrumentalities that are under his control—that is, the army and navy. It is for this purpose that an army and navy are kept constantly on hand, in times of peace as well as in times of war, of which the President himself, by the provisions of the Constitution, is at all times the Commander-in-Chief.

Whenever and wherever, then, in times of peace or in times of war, in loyal or disloyal districts, there are combinations or influences tending to the destruction of the laws, and which the Courts can not or do not control, the President is to employ this army or navy, or both, as the case requires. And when he does so, to arrest and imprison those who are instigating or waging war against the laws, is the very mildest form certainly, that he can possibly deal with them consistent with his duty and the safety of the country; and if the insurgents are too numerous to be kept under in this manner, his plain duty is to engage in a very timely use of bayonets and bullets.

Now, had the President of the United States performed this simple, plain, constitutional duty, at the first instigation of this rebellion, and been sustained in it by all who were really loyal at heart, the rebellion would never have gained any dangerous character. The timorous fears inspired in the hearts of loyal men, by the *hue and cry* of traitors, against the exercise by the President of his constitutional powers for suppressing this rebellion, is the chief hand-maid of the rebellion itself, that first helped it into existence, and has nourished it from its birth. But after all, this distrust of the President, and this fettering of his hands by popular influences, while the enemies of the Government are preying upon its vitals, is but an infraction of the great fundamental law of the sovereignty of the constitutional majority already discussed.

WHO IS ACCOUNTABLE FOR THE REBELLION.

We have heard much controversy in reference to the responsibity of this rebellion. Some charge it upon the Republican party, others upon the Democratic; some say it is upon the people of the North, others upon those of the South, and a variety of other opinions are held. Whoever is responsible for the destruction of free speech, the purity of elections and the sovereignty of the majority, is responsible for the rebellion. Judging by this rule, very few of us, if any, will wholly escape. Let us consider this matter. First, let us see who is accountable for the destruction of the freedom of speech.

It is true, the Southern people have committed the outrages by which our national freedom of speech was destroyed. But in this country, wherein every citizen is a sovereign, men are not only responsible for what they do, but for what they neglect to do. For thirty or forty years this destruction of free speech has been going on constantly, with the full knowledge of every citizen in the nation, the people have all the time had in their hands the plain constitutional power to prevent it at any time. And now the question arises, who is there that has done any thing towards this object? What party, in any section of the country, has proposed and urged, at any time, the proper constitutional appliance to stay this destruction? If any party has ever done this, the fact has not come to the knowledge of the writer. There are, or have been, parties that have said much in platforms, resolutions and orations, in extolling the right of free speech, but those who have dwelt most in this strain have most completely ignored the fact of its notorious violation and destruction. Many of the Northern people have indulged freely in the use of harsh epithets towards these Southern people, for destroying this freedom of speech, and more especially for the outrages upon persons and property that have been resorted to for the accomplishment of the purpose, but these epithets constitute no remedy for the evil— none in the least.

In reference to the purity of elections, so far as this has been destroyed by violent means in the Slave States, the responsibility rests in all respects precisely with that for the destruction of free speech, because accomplished by the same species of violence on the part of the Southern people, and the same criminal neglect on the part of the Northern. But so far as the purity of elections has been destroyed by threats of insurrection, the people of the North and South are almost equally culpable for it. Because this argument of danger to the Union, has been used in commonever ywhere— North as well as South—and everywhere the people have been more or less corrupted by it.

So in respect to the subversion of the sovereignty of the majority; the people of the North and South have in common aided each other in the accomplishment of this purpose. The three great compromises of the country, each of which was but the result of a separate and distinct contest for supremacy between the majority and minority, in which the former bowed in humble submission to the latter, were supported in Congress by the representatives of the North as well as the South, and acquiesced in by their constituencies at home, and more or less by all parties.

Moreover, in the early stages of the rebellion, when a number of the States were hesitating in reference to the question

5

of any State or Territory, or to hold property. For when the mass of the people of the rebellious States, under the benign influence of free speech, shall learn how terribly they have been misled and deceived by their leaders, those leaders will be consigned to an infamy lower, and more to be dreaded, than the grave itself.

OUR TRUST MUST BE IN GOD.

After all that is said, or can be said, it is not in the wisdom of man alone to preserve this nation. As a people we have been established by Him, whose ways are above our ways. It is to the God of the Bible, the Creator of all things, that we are indebted for our goodly heritage, our miraculous preservation, and an unrivalled prosperity. A nation thus favored must not forget its benefactor. We must be essentially a religious people or no people. Precisely to the extent that we trust in our own strength alone, God will disclose our weakness. In proportion as we discard his laws, he will render ours of no avail; and in proportion as we reject his counsels, he will divide, confound and bring to naught, ours.

In the darkest days of the revolution, when General Washington was charged with his weightiest cares, anxieties and labors, he did not leave all the praying to be done by his chaplains, but he himself raised his own voice and hands in supplication of that help that no human power could afford. Why, then, should it be thought a thing beneath the dignity, or time or talents of our President, our Senators, Representatives and Judges to do the same? Upon each man, whatever may be his rank or condition in life, rests a religious obligation that no one else can discharge for him.

We must not only be a praying people, but we must have the true spirit of christianity. We must fear God, and not mock him with vain oblations, whilst our hearts are full of extortion, excess and all manner of perverseness. In all our relations, public and private, we must deal justly, love mercy, and walk humbly with God; so shall our days be prolonged in the land which the Lord our God has given us.